Success With Addition & Subtraction

D1398246

New York • Toronto • London • Auckland • Sydney
Mexico City • New Delhi • Hong Kong • Buenos Aires

Teaching *Resources*

State Standards Correlations

To find out how this book helps you meet your state's standards, log on to **www.scholastic.com/ssw**

Written by Danette Randolph
Cover design by Ka-Yeon Kim-Li
Interior illustrations by Sherry Neidigh
Interior design by Quack & Company

ISBN 978-0-545-20098-1

18 19 20   40   22 21 20

Introduction

Parents and teachers alike will find **Addition & Subtraction** to be a valuable learning tool. Children will enjoy completing a wide variety of math activities that are both engaging and educational. Take a look at the Table of Contents and you will feel rewarded providing such a valuable resource for your children. Remember to praise children for their efforts and successes!

Table of Contents

Clowning Around

Color Code

1	pink
2	white
3	black
4	brown
5	purple
6	green
7	blue
8	orange
9	yellow
10	red

$$4 + 5$$

$$5 + 0$$

$$5 + 2 =$$

$$6 + 3 =$$

$$2 + 3$$

$$7 + 2$$

$$4 + 4$$

$$2 + 5 =$$

$$3 + 2 =$$

$$4 + 3$$

$$3 + 3$$

$$1 + 0$$

$$4 + 2$$

$$0 + 1$$

$$5 + 1$$

$$4 + 1 =$$

$$6 + 2$$

$$2 + 1$$

$$3 + 0$$

$$3 + 5$$

$$7 + 0 =$$

$$5 + 5 =$$

$$6 + 1 =$$

$$1 + 1$$

$$7 + 3 =$$

$$3 + 1 =$$

Lovely Ladybugs

Write a number sentence to show how many spots each ladybug has.

1 + 2 = 3

2 + 3 = 5

3 + 7 = 10

4 + 3 = 7

1 + 0 = 1

3 + 2 = 5

1 + 1 = 2

4 + 4 = 8

1 + 3 = 4

Color the ladybug with the greatest number of spots red.

Color the ladybug with the least number of spots blue.

Beautiful Bouquet

Look at the number on each bow. Draw more flowers to match the number written on the bow.

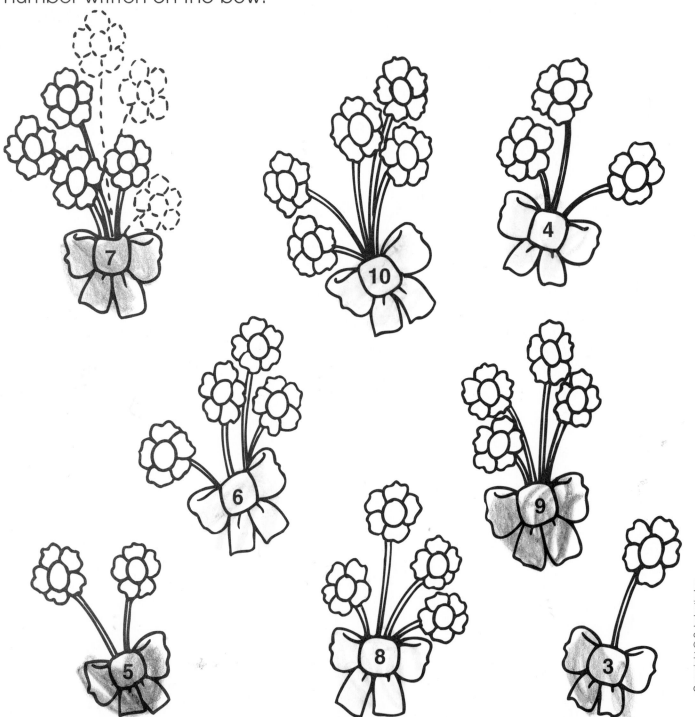

 Color the bows with an even number yellow.
Color the bows with an odd number purple.

Night Lights

Subtract. Connect
the dots from
greatest to least.

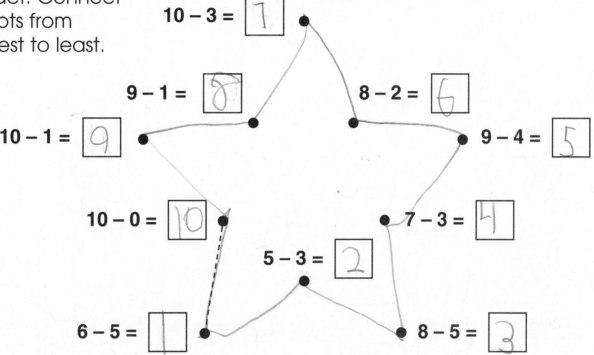

10 – 3 = [7]

9 – 1 = [8]   8 – 2 = [6]

10 – 1 = [9]   9 – 4 = [5]

10 – 0 = [10]   7 – 3 = [4]

5 – 3 = [2]

6 – 5 = [1]   8 – 5 = [3]

Subtract.
Connect the
dots from least
to greatest.

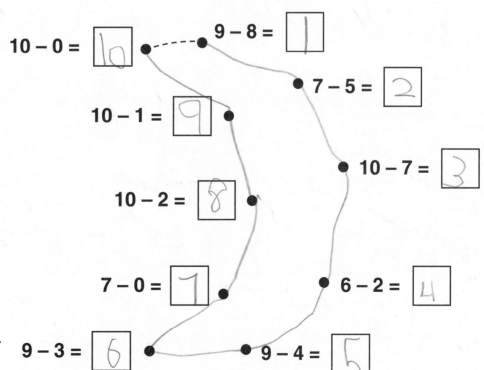

10 – 0 = [10]   9 – 8 = [1]

7 – 5 = [2]

10 – 1 = [9]

10 – 7 = [3]

10 – 2 = [8]

7 – 0 = [7]   6 – 2 = [4]

9 – 3 = [6]   9 – 4 = [5]

**The top picture
gives off its own
light. Color this
picture orange.
The bottom
picture reflects
light from the sun.
Color this picture
yellow.**

Hop to It

Add or subtract. Trace the number line with your finger to check your work.

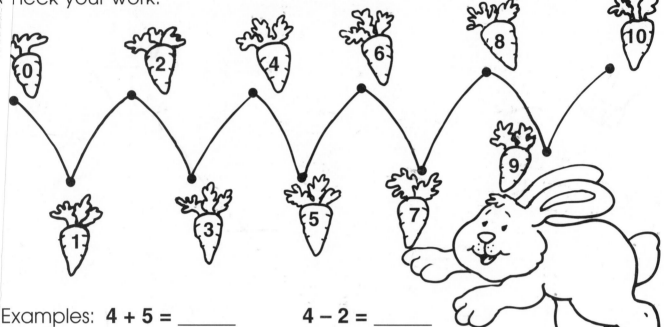

Examples: **4 + 5 = _____**   **4 − 2 = _____**

Start on **4**.   Start on **4**.

Move **5** 🥕 right.   Move **2** 🥕 left.

7 − 3 = _____	**9 − 6 = _____**	**2 + 0 = _____**
5 + 5 = _____	**8 − 7 = _____**	**4 + 3 = _____**
10 − 4 = _____	**6 + 2 = _____**	**7 − 2 = _____**

 Circle the answer to each question.

What direction did **move to add?   left   or   right**

What direction did **move to subtract?   left   or   right**

Mitten Matchup

Add or subtract. Draw a line to match mittens with the same answer.

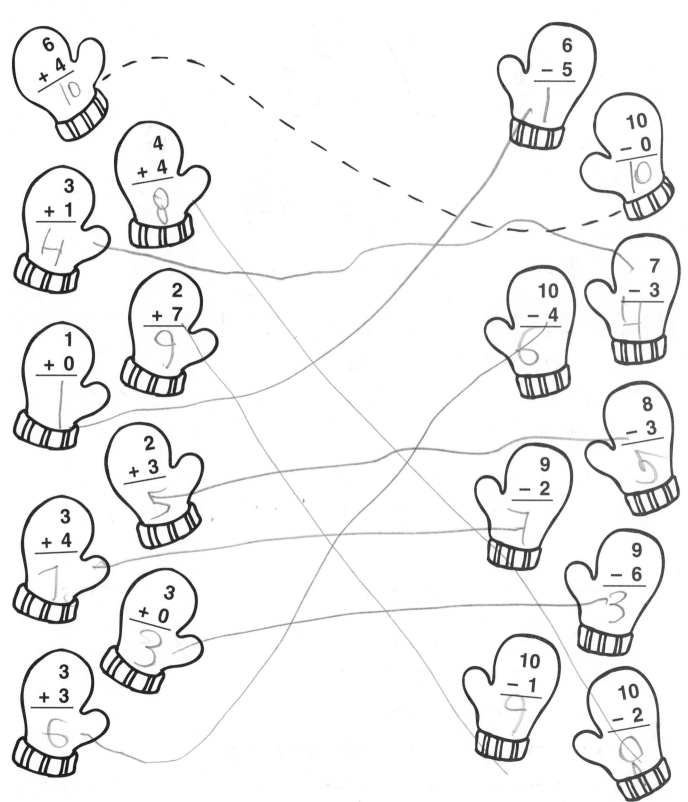

Blast Off

Add or subtract. Then use the code to answer the riddle below.

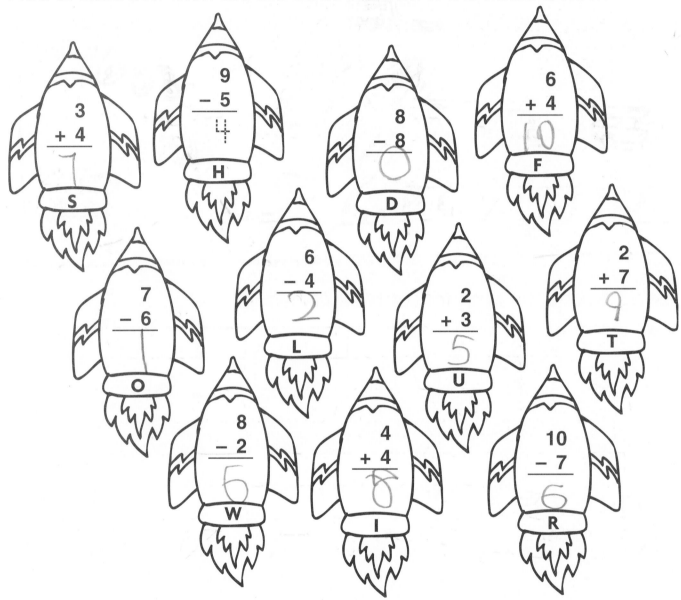

3 + 4 = 7 **S**

9 − 5 = 4 **H**

8 − 8 = 0 **D**

6 + 4 = 10 **F**

7 − 6 = 1 **O**

6 − 4 = 2 **L**

2 + 3 = 5 **U**

2 + 7 = 9 **T**

8 − 2 = 6 **W**

4 + 4 = 8 **I**

10 − 7 = 3 **R**

How is an astronaut's job unlike any other job?

I I' S   O U T   O F
8 9 7   1 5 9   1 10

T H I S   W O R L D !
9 4 8 7   6 1 3 2 0

Out on the Town

Color a box on the graph for each item in the picture.

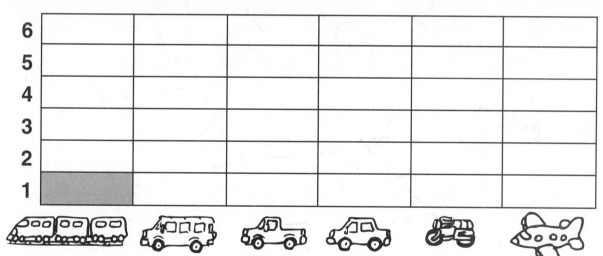

A. How many  and ✈ altogether? $\underline{6}$ $\oplus$ $\underline{2}$ $=$ $\underline{8}$

B. How many 🏍 and 🚆 in all?   ___ + ___ = ___
                                          −

C. How many more 🚗 than 🚌 ?   ___ + ___ = ___
                                          −

Shapes on a Snake

Add or subtract.

A. + = 10

B. 10 - 5 = 5 / 10

C. 9 - 2 = 7

D. 4 + 6 = 5 / 10

E. 7 + 2 = 9

F. 2 + 3 = 5

G. 5 + 3 = 8

H. 6 + 4 = 10

I. 8 - 7 = 1

J. 10 - 3 = 7

Leap on Over

Add. To show the frog's path across the pond, color each lily pad green if the sum is greater than 10.

10 + 1 = 11

6 + 4 = 10

6 + 9 = 15

5 + 2 = 7

7 + 0 = 7

5 + 5 = 10

9 + 2 = 11

10 + 4 = 14

3 + 7 = 10

5 + 4 = 9

7 + 6 = 13

4 + 3 = 7

3 + 8 = 11

2 + 2 = 4

8 + 8 = 16

How many leaps did the frog take across the pond? _____

Name _____

Flying High

Add down and across to find the missing number.

A.

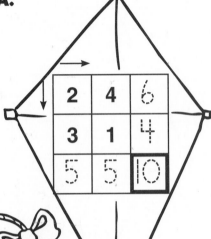

2	4	6
3	1	4
5	5	10

B.

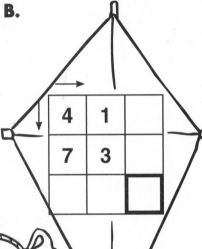

4	1	
7	3	

C.

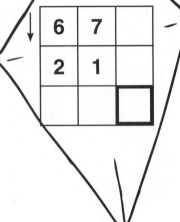

6	7	
2	1	

D.

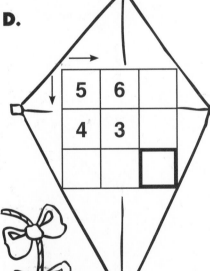

5	6	
4	3	

E.

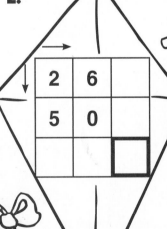

2	6	
5	0	

F.

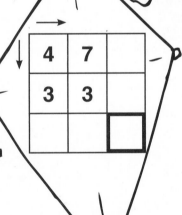

4	7	
3	3	

Double Dips

Write the doubles that equal the number on the cone.

8
8
16

4
4
8

6
6
12

8
8
16

1
1
2

3
3
6

9
9
18

2
2
4

5
5
10

7
7
14

Circle the answer.

When adding doubles, the sum will always be: even   odd

Not Far From Home

Start at  .Write the number of steps. Add.

steps to + steps home = _____ steps	steps to + steps home = _____ steps

Break the Code

Subtract.

A. 6
   – 2

B. 13
   – 7
○

C. 17
   – 7
▭

D. 18
   – 9

E. 15
   – 8
◇

F. 11
   – 9
▢

G. 9
   – 4
⬡

H. 14
   – 6
○

I. 11
   – 8
⬢

J. 7
   – 6
▽

Use the answers above to solve each problem.

K.

▢
– ___

L.
⬠
⬢
– ___

M.
◇
⬡
– ___

N.
○
▽
– ___

O.

○
– ___

P.
▽ ○
○
– ___

Q.
▽ △
⬡
– ___

Name _____

The Big Search

Subtract. Circle the difference.

11 – 7 = five three (four)	**14 – 9 =** nine one five
13 – 6 = six nine seven	**16 – 5 =** twelve thirteen eleven
18 – 9 = eleven ten nine	**17 – 11 =** seven six ten
15 – 5 = ten seven five	**12 – 9 =** three two four
12 – 4 = six eight nine	**11 – 9 =** three five two

Find each circled number in the word puzzle. Look → and ↓.

```
(f  o  u  r)  h  i  o  n  e  g  s  k  m
 i  f  o  n  t  g  y  f  a  f  u  e  z
 f  t  l  u  e  j  s  i  x  s  b  x  t
 t  t  w  e  l  v  e  v  k  s  t  l  h
 e  p  n  i  n  e  w  e  j  e  r  t  i
 e  d  n  g  q  i  h  r  y  v  a  q  r
 n  v  h  h  o  t  h  r  e  e  c  s  t
 d  m  k  t  c  w  b  t  e  n  t  r  e
 x  d  i  p  g  o  a  c  p  f  i  s  e
 c  e  l  e  v  e  n  a  b  z  o  v  n
 b  w  u  d  i  f  f  e  r  e  n  c  e
```

 See if you can find these number words: twelve, fifteen, thirteen, subtraction, difference.

Race Through the Facts

Add or subtract. The race car that ends with the highest number wins the race!

7 + 2 = ___   − 4 = ___   − 3 = ___   + 9 = ___

12 − 3 = ___   − 6 = ___   + 2 = ___   + 9 = ___   + 5 = ___   − 8 = ___

− 9 = ___   + 7 = ___   − 6 = ___   + 3 = ___   − 2 = ___   + 7 = ___

+ 4 = ___   + 6 = ___   + 1 = ___   + 4 = ___

+ 1 = ___   − 8 = ___   + 2 = ___   + 3 = ___   − 3 = ___

− 11 = ___   − 5 = ___   + 13 = ___   − 7 = ___   + 3 = ___

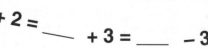

 Color the winning race car blue.

Little Snacks

Add or subtract. Then follow the maze through the even answers.

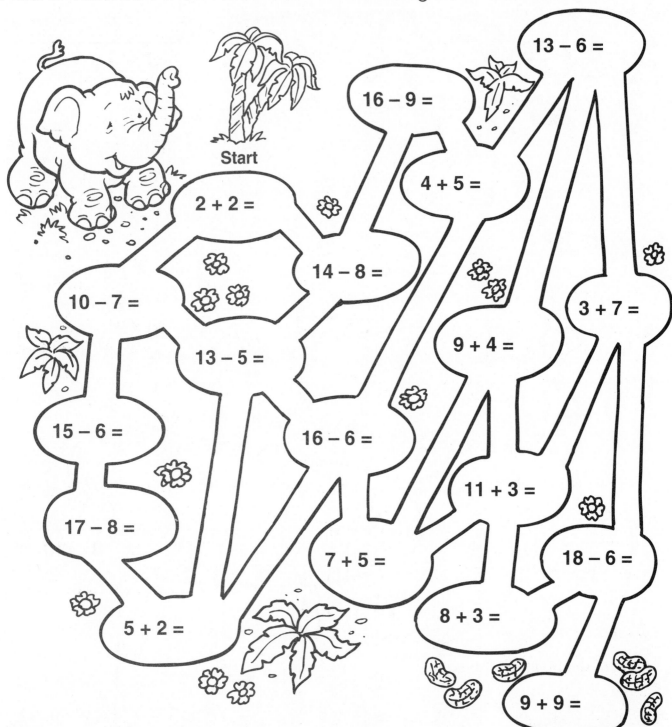

Start

16 − 9 =

13 − 6 =

4 + 5 =

2 + 2 =

14 − 8 =

10 − 7 =

3 + 7 =

13 − 5 =

9 + 4 =

15 − 6 =

16 − 6 =

17 − 8 =

11 + 3 =

7 + 5 =

18 − 6 =

8 + 3 =

5 + 2 =

9 + 9 =

 The elephant found 9 peanuts. He ate 6 peanuts.

How many peanuts are left? _____

Flying Families

Fill in the missing number for each family. Use the numbers from the box.

9	12	15	8	10
6	4	7	5	11	2

💡 **Fill in the families with twins.**

Colorful Flowers

Color a box on the graph for each item in the picture.

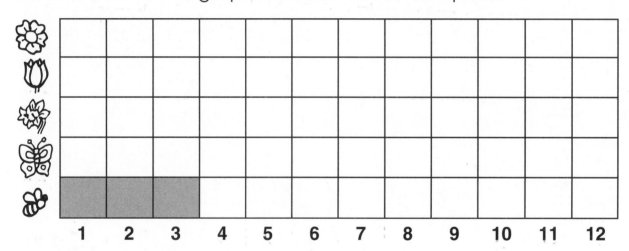

| | 1 | 2 | 3 | 4 | 5 | 6 | 7 | 8 | 9 | 10 | 11 | 12 |

A. Which flower is found the most?

B. How many and altogether? _____ + _____ = _____

C. How many more than  ? _____ – _____ = _____

D. How many insects in all? _____ + _____ = _____

E. How many more  than ? _____ – _____ = _____

F. How many and  altogether? _____ + _____ = _____

A Perfect Strike

Fill in the missing number.

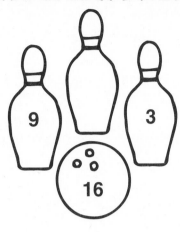

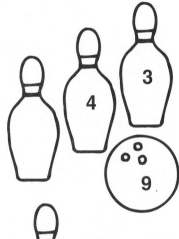

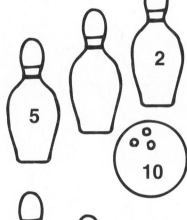

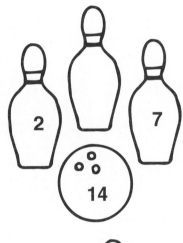

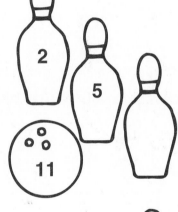

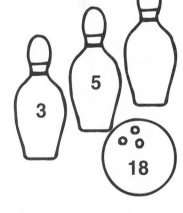

Find three different ways to make 8 with 3 numbers.

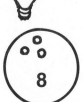

Name _____

What a Treat!

Find the number in the mouse and cheese. ☐

Find the sum of the numbers in the cheese.

_____ + _____ + _____ = _____

Find the sum of the numbers in the mouse.

_____ + _____ + _____ = _____

Find the number in the rabbit and carrot. ☐

Find the sum of the largest number in the rabbit and the smallest number in the carrot.

_____ + _____ = _____

Find the difference between the largest and smallest number in the carrot.

_____ − _____ = _____

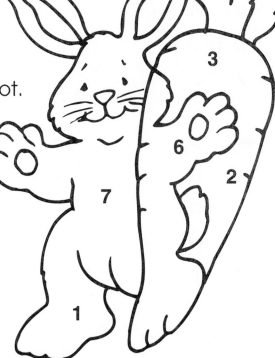

 Find the sum of all the numbers in the mouse and cheese.

_____ + _____ + _____ + _____ + _____ = _____

Find the sum of all the numbers in the rabbit and carrot.

_____ + _____ + _____ + _____ + _____ = _____

Have a Heart

Circle a group of 10. Write the number of tens and ones.

tens	ones

tens	ones

tens	ones

tens	ones

tens	ones

tens	ones

tens	ones

tens	ones

Beautiful Butterflies

Add. Color the picture using the color code.

Color Code

26	red
29	orange
38	green
54	purple
87	yellow

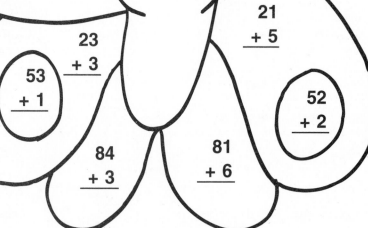

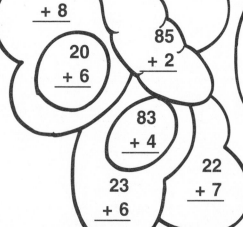

Most adult butterflies live for about
```
  11
+  3
```
days.

Where's the Beach?

Add. To find the path to the beach, color each box with an odd answer yellow.

	14 + 3	34 + 2	81 + 3

76 + 2	25 + 4	56 + 3	11 + 3	40 + 8
87 + 1	22 + 2	32 + 3	65 + 1	93 + 5
10 + 8	41 + 2	70 + 7	32 + 6	84 + 4
73 + 5	63 + 2	55 + 1	41 + 5	23 + 3

	98 + 1	53 + 4	82 + 5

By the Seashore

Use the code below to write each missing number. Add.

93
+ _____

82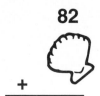
+ _____

14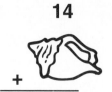
+ _____

21
+ _____

53
+ _____

45
+ _____

73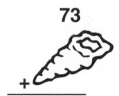
+ _____

36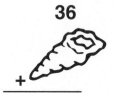
+ _____

61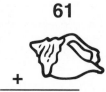
+ _____

32
+ _____

 Find the sum for all the shells. _____ + _____ + _____ + _____ + _____ = _____

Sail Away

Finish each addition sentence. Add.

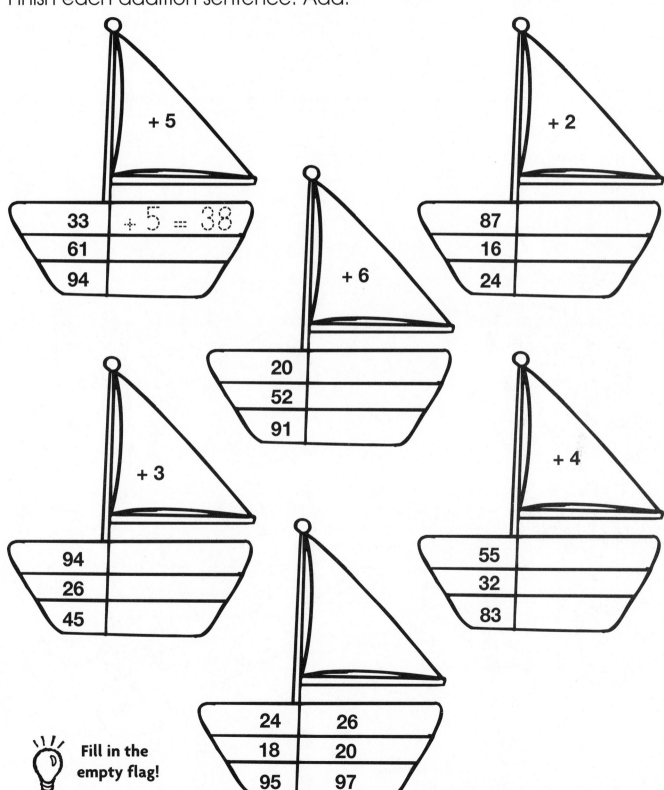

+ 5

33	+ 5 = 38
61	
94	

+ 6

| 20 |
| 52 |
| 91 |

+ 2

| 87 |
| 16 |
| 24 |

+ 3

| 94 |
| 26 |
| 45 |

+ 4

| 55 |
| 32 |
| 83 |

24	26
18	20
95	97

Fill in the empty flag!

Name _____

Dino-Math

Subtract. Color the picture using the color code.

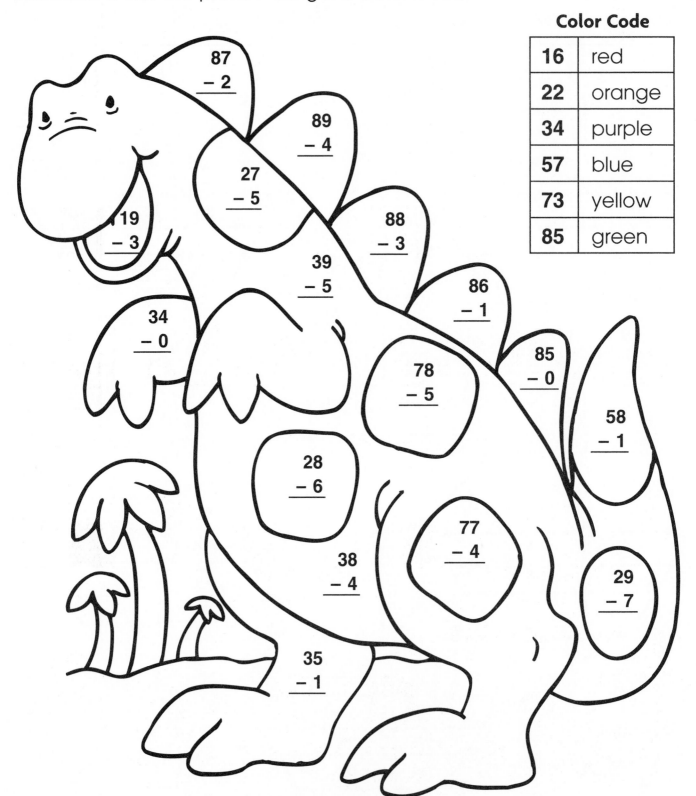

Color Code

16	red
22	orange
34	purple
57	blue
73	yellow
85	green

Number Buddies

Subtract. Remember: the largest number always goes on top!

A.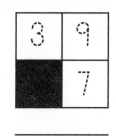

B.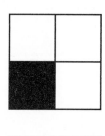

C.

D.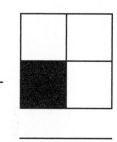

E.

F.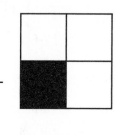

G.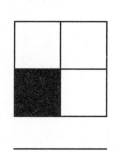

H.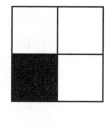

 Fill in each missing number.

   35

   20

   83

Treasure Island

Subtract.

43 − 1	95 − 5	79 − 3	36 − 4	89 − 7	66 − 3	83 − 2
59 − 9	37 − 2	24 − 3	27 − 6	42 − 1	90 − 0	55 − 2
33 − 3	84 − 4	28 − 8	71 − 1	62 − 2	68 − 3	77 − 3

Use the clues to find the gold, the ship, and the treasure in the boxes above.

Find the gold.
The difference is greater than **50** and less than **55**. Color the box with the gold yellow.

Find the ship.
The difference is greater than **30** and less than **35**. Color the box with the ship orange.

Find the sunken treasure.
The difference is greater than **70** and less than **75**. Color the box with the treasure red.

Riding on Air

Add. Color the picture using the color code.

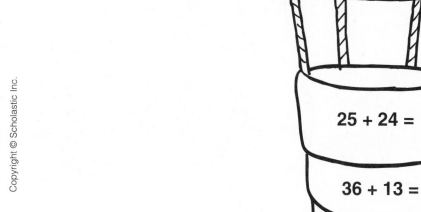

Color Code	
24	red
37	blue
49	brown
54	white
78	yellow
86	purple
95	green

42
+ 53

31
+ 23

46
+ 32

24 + 13 =

24
+ 62

23
+ 55

64
+ 14

60
+ 18

65
+ 21

75
+ 11

53
+ 33

24
+ 30

15 + 22 =

11 + 13 =

42
+ 12

54
+ 32

42
+ 36

15
+ 22

72 + 23 =

25 + 24 =

36 + 13 =

37 + 12 =

Have a Ball

Subtract.

39
− 12

97
− 23

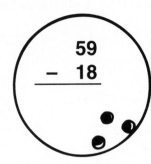
59
− 18

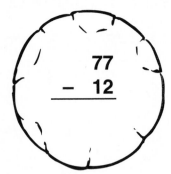
77
− 12

79
− 52

81
− 11

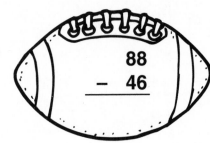
88
− 46

63
− 10

58
− 43

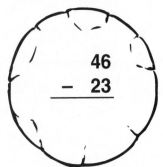
46
− 23

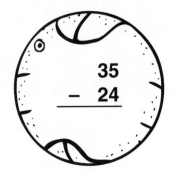
35
− 24

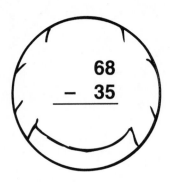
68
− 35

32
− 12

74
− 72

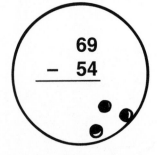
69
− 54

83
− 52

 The Rams scored 49 points in the football game. The Bears scored 27 points.

How many more points did the Rams score than the Bears? _____

Opposites Attract

Add or subtract. Connect the magnets that have the same answer.

42
+ 33

 new

close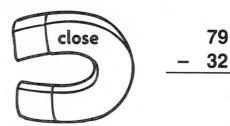

79
− 32

32
+ 54

 laugh

old

99
− 24

35
+ 12

 open

left

99
− 10

13
+ 10

 sink

cry

98
− 12

37
+ 52

 right

float

48
− 25

 On another sheet of paper, write an addition and subtraction problem which have the same answer.

How Much Money?

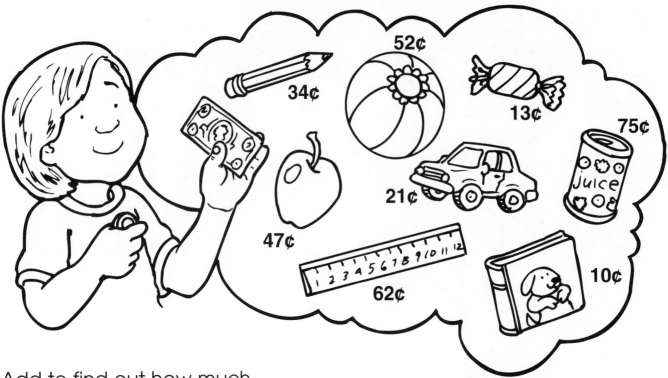

Add to find out how much.

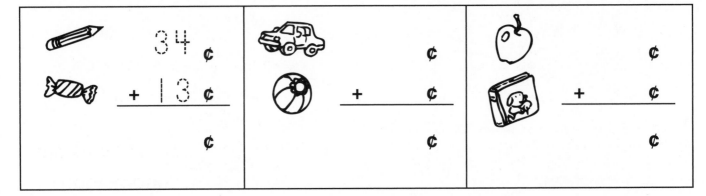

Subtract to find out how much.

Snuggle Up With a Book

Day of the Week	Reading Minutes
Sunday	97
Monday	28
Tuesday	73
Wednesday	44
Thursday	51
Friday	45
Saturday	80

Use the chart to answer the questions.

A. What day did Alex read for the longest time?

_____

B. How many minutes did Alex read on Wednesday and Friday? _____ minutes

C. What day did Alex read for the shortest time?

_____

D. How many more minutes did Alex read on Sunday than Tuesday? _____ minutes

E. How many minutes did Alex read on Monday and Thursday? _____ minutes

F. How many more minutes did Alex read on Tuesday than Thursday? _____ minutes

 One hour is 60 minutes. On what days did Alex read longer than one hour?

_____, _____, _____

Let the Sun Shine

Add or subtract. Then use the code to fill in the letters to finish each sun fact.

13	26	34	42	57	63	71	76	85	88
f	a	s	g	r	e	l	h	t	i

$$\begin{array}{r} 13 \\ +\ 21 \\ \hline \end{array} \qquad \begin{array}{r} 32 \\ +\ 53 \\ \hline \end{array} \qquad \begin{array}{r} 57 \\ -\ 31 \\ \hline \end{array} \qquad \begin{array}{r} 89 \\ -\ 32 \\ \hline \end{array}$$

The sun is a ____ ____ ____ ____.

$$\begin{array}{r} 30 \\ +\ 41 \\ \hline \end{array} \qquad \begin{array}{r} 98 \\ -\ 10 \\ \hline \end{array} \qquad \begin{array}{r} 12 \\ +\ 30 \\ \hline \end{array} \qquad \begin{array}{r} 97 \\ -\ 21 \\ \hline \end{array} \qquad \begin{array}{r} 99 \\ -\ 14 \\ \hline \end{array}$$

The sun gives ____ ____ ____ ____ ____ and

$$\begin{array}{r} 34 \\ +\ 42 \\ \hline \end{array} \qquad \begin{array}{r} 51 \\ +\ 12 \\ \hline \end{array} \qquad \begin{array}{r} 88 \\ -\ 62 \\ \hline \end{array} \qquad \begin{array}{r} 42 \\ +\ 43 \\ \hline \end{array}$$

____ ____ ____ ____ to Earth.

$$\begin{array}{r} 88 \\ -\ 17 \\ \hline \end{array} \qquad \begin{array}{r} 56 \\ +\ 32 \\ \hline \end{array} \qquad \begin{array}{r} 49 \\ -\ 36 \\ \hline \end{array} \qquad \begin{array}{r} 30 \\ +\ 33 \\ \hline \end{array}$$

Without the sun, there would be no ____ ____ ____ ____.

Animal Surprises

Add or subtract. Match the answer to the animal fact.

$$\begin{array}{r} 47 \\ +\ 32 \\ \hline \end{array}$$

wild boar

$$\begin{array}{r} 22 \\ +\ 56 \\ \hline \end{array}$$

ostrich

$$\begin{array}{r} 65 \\ -\ 34 \\ \hline \end{array}$$

bat

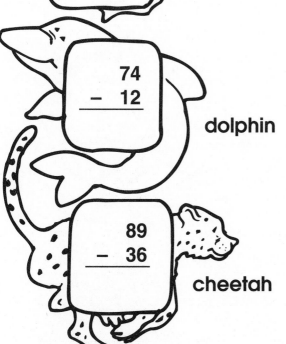

$$\begin{array}{r} 74 \\ -\ 12 \\ \hline \end{array}$$

dolphin

$$\begin{array}{r} 89 \\ -\ 36 \\ \hline \end{array}$$

cheetah

31 I am the only mammal that can fly.

78 I am a large bird, but I cannot fly.

79 I can weigh over 250 pounds.

53 I am the fastest of all animals.

62 I swim like a fish, but I am really a mammal.

Fishbowl Families

Add or subtract. Circle the fish that
does not belong with the family.
Hint: Look at the tens place.

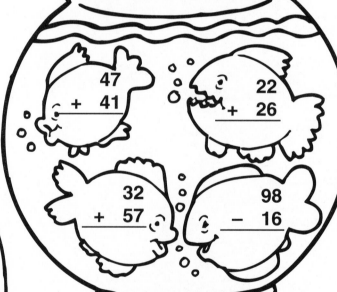

$$\begin{array}{r} 37 \\ +\ 12 \\ \hline \end{array} \qquad \begin{array}{r} 96 \\ -\ 51 \\ \hline \end{array}$$

$$\begin{array}{r} 83 \\ -\ 40 \\ \hline \end{array} \qquad \begin{array}{r} 23 \\ +\ 64 \\ \hline \end{array}$$

$$\begin{array}{r} 42 \\ +\ 23 \\ \hline \end{array} \qquad \begin{array}{r} 33 \\ 36 \\ \hline \end{array}$$

$$\begin{array}{r} 27 \\ +\ 12 \\ \hline \end{array} \qquad \begin{array}{r} 51 \\ +\ 13 \\ \hline \end{array}$$

$$\begin{array}{r} 47 \\ +\ 41 \\ \hline \end{array} \qquad \begin{array}{r} 22 \\ +\ 26 \\ \hline \end{array}$$

$$\begin{array}{r} 32 \\ +\ 57 \\ \hline \end{array} \qquad \begin{array}{r} 98 \\ -\ 16 \\ \hline \end{array}$$

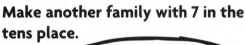 **Make another family with 7 in the
tens place.**

Page 4

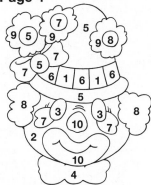

Check child's coloring.

Page 5

1 + 2 = 3, 2 + 3 = 5, 7 + 3 = 10; 3 + 4 = 7, 1 + 0 = 1, 3 + 2 = 5; 1 + 1 = 2, 4 + 4 = 8; 1 + 3 = 4; The ladybug with 10 spots should be colored red. The ladybug with 1 spot should be colored blue.

Page 6

Check that the child has drawn the correct number of flowers. 7: needs 3, 10: needs 5, 4: needs 1; 6: needs 2, 9: needs 5; 5: needs 3, 8: needs 4, 3: needs 2; Color the bows with the numbers 4, 6, 8, and 10 yellow. Color the bows with 3, 5, 7, and 9 purple.

Page 7

2, 3, 2; 3, 2, 1

Page 8

Check child's coloring.

Page 9

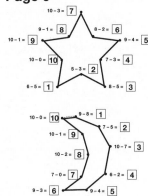

Page 10

4, 3, 2; 10, 1, 7; 6, 8, 5; The rabbit moved right to add. The rabbit moved left to subtract.

Page 11

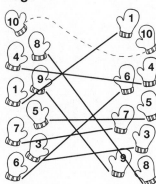

Page 12

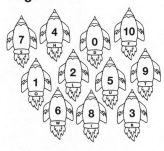

IT'S OUT OF THIS WORLD!

Page 13

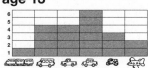

A. 6 + 2 = 8; B. 3 + 1 = 4; C. 6 − 4 = 2

Page 14

A. 6 + 4 = 10; B. 10 − 5 = 5; C. 9 − 2 = 7; D. 4 + 6 = 10; E. 7 + 2 = 9; F. 2 + 3 = 5; G. 5 + 3 = 8; H. 6 + 2 = 8; I. 8 − 7 = 1; J. 10 − 3 = 7

Page 15

A. 7 + 3 = 10; B. 7 − 4 = 3; C. 10 − 6 = 4; D. 8 − 2 = 6; E. 5 + 4 = 9

Page 16

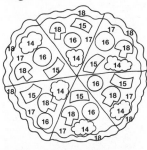

Check child's coloring.; 11 ways; 0 + 10 = 10, 1 + 9 = 10, 2 + 8 = 10, 3 + 7 = 10, 4 + 6 = 10, 5 + 5 = 10, 6 + 4 = 10, 7 + 3 = 10, 8 + 2 = 10, 9 + 1 = 10, 10 + 0 = 10

Page 17

7 leaps

Page 18

A.
2	4	6
3	1	4
5	5	10

B.
4	1	5
7	3	10
11	4	15

C.
6	7	13
2	1	3
8	8	16

D.
5	6	11
4	3	7
9	9	18

E.
2	6	8
5	0	5
7	6	13

F.
4	7	11
3	3	6
7	10	17

Page 19

8, 8; 4, 4; 6, 6; 8, 8; 1, 1; 3, 3; 9, 9; 2, 2; 5, 5; 7, 7; even

Page 20

7 + 7 = 14, 5 + 5 = 10, 8 + 8 = 16, 6 + 6 = 12; 9 + 9 = 18, 3 + 3 = 6, 2 + 2 = 4; 4 + 4 = 8

Page 21

A. 4; B. 6; C. 10; D. 9; E. 7; F. 2; G. 5; H. 8; I. 3; J. 1; K. 5 − 2 = 3; L. 9 − 3 = 6; M. 7 − 5 = 2; N. 8 − 1 = 7; O. 12 − 6 = 6; P. 16 − 8 = 8; Q. 14 − 5 = 9

Page 22

four, five; seven, eleven; nine, six; ten, three; eight, two

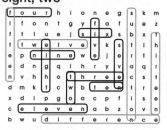

Page 23

7 + 2 = 9 − 4 = 5 − 3 = 2 + 9 = 11 + 5 = 16 − 8 = 8 + 4 = 12 + 6 = 18 − 9 = 9 + 1 = 10 + 4 = 14 − 8 = 6 + 2 = 8 + 3 = 11 − 3 = 8; 12 − 3 = 9 − 6 = 3 + 2 = 5 + 9 = 14 − 6 = 8 + 7 = 15 − 6 = 9 + 3 = 12 − 2 = 10 + 7 = 17 + 1 = 18 − 11 = 7 − 5 = 2 + 13 = 15 − 7 = 8 + 3 = 11; Color the bottom car blue.

Page 24

3 peanuts

Page 25

3, 3; 7, 7; 9, 9; 5, 5; 8, 8

Page 26

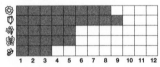

A. First flower should be circled.; B. 8 + 9 = 17; C. 5 − 5 = 0; D. 5 + 3 = 8; E. 5 − 3 = 2; F. 9 + 5 = 14

Page 27

A. 13, 12, 13, 13; B. 12, 11, 11, 11; C. 17, 15, 15, 17; D. 14, 14, 14, 16
Check child's coloring.

Page 28

- 1; 12, 11, 10, 9, 8, 7
+2; 2, 4, 6, 8, 10, 12
+3; 3, 6, 9, 12, 15, 18
-2; 13, 11, 9, 7, 5, 3

Page 29

2, 4, 2; 3, 5, 4; 6, 4, 10;
Answers will vary.

Page 30

5; 3 + 2 + 5 = 10; 4 + 5 + 7 = 16; 6; 7 + 2 = 9; 6 − 2 = 4; 7 + 4 + 5 + 3 + 2 = 21; 1 + 7 + 6 + 3 + 2 = 19

Page 31

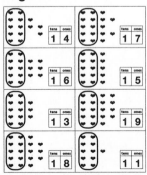

Page 32

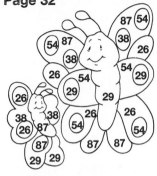

Check child's coloring;
14 days

Page 33

Page 34

93 + 6 = 99, 82 + 4 = 86, 14 + 5 = 19, 21 + 7 = 28, 53 + 6 = 59; 45 + 4 = 49, 73 + 3 = 76, 36 + 3 = 39, 61 + 5 = 66, 32 + 7 = 39; 4 + 7 + 5 + 3 + 6 = 25

Page 35

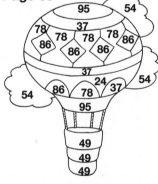

Page 36

Check child's coloring.

Page 37

A. 39 − 7 = 32; B. 54 − 1 = 53; C. 87 − 6 = 81; D. 73 − 3 = 70; E. 25 − 4 = 21; F. 42 − 2 = 40; G. 98 − 7 = 91; H. 66 − 5 = 61; 4, 7, 5

Page 38

42, 90, 76, 32, 82, 63, 81; 50, 35, 21, 21, 41, 90, 53; 30, 80, 20, 70, 60, 65, 74; The box with 53 should be colored yellow. The box with 32 should be colored orange. The box with 74 should be colored red.

Page 39

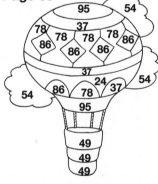

Check child's coloring.

Page 40

27, 74, 41, 65; 27, 70, 42, 53; 15, 23, 11, 33; 20, 2, 15, 31; 22

Page 41

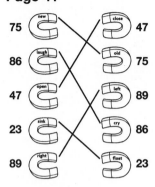

Answers will vary.

Page 42

34 + 13 = 47, 21 + 52 = 73, 47 + 10 = 57; 75 − 34 = 41, 62 − 21 = 41, 47 − 13 = 34

Page 43

A. Sunday; B. 89; C. Monday; D. 24; E. 79; F. 22; Sunday, Tuesday, Saturday

Page 44

34, 85, 26, 57; star; 71, 88, 42, 76, 85; light; 76, 63, 26, 85; heat; 71, 88, 13, 63; life

Page 45

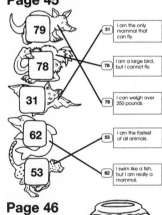

Page 46

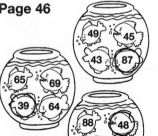

Answers will vary.